WHY WOULD ANYONE WEAR THAT?

FASCINATING FASHION FACTS

Written by Celia E. Stall-Meadows
Illustrated by Leslie Stall Widener

intellect Bristol, UK / Chicago, USA

ACKNOWLEDGMENTS

This beautifully illustrated book is for anyone who is intrigued by fashion. While costume history students learn a vast amount about apparel from prehistoric times to the present, *Why Would Anyone Wear That? Fascinating Fashion Facts* presents discussions of only the most extreme clothing items.

We would like to express our sincere thanks to the following people at Intellect: Bethan Ball, production manager, and Melanie Marshall, assistant book publisher, for their guidance and generous support; and James Campbell, marketing executive, who attended the ITAA conference and made the initial contact.

FROM CELIA STALL-MEADOWS

Thank you to my former professors at Oklahoma State University for enriching my understanding of this subject matter. The costume history class I took as an undergraduate initially fostered my interest; later, I completed a graduate assistantship as the curator for OSU's historic costume collection. When teaching university courses in history of costume, I discovered that learners are not only interested in *what* people wore, but in *why* people wore these clothing extremes. A special thank you goes to my talented sister, Leslie, whose precise illustrations are truly worth a thousand words. May this be the beginning of many more book collaborations. To our supportive and loving parents, Joe C. and Jo A. Stall, we are sure this will be your coffee table book. To my husband, Kendall, and our children, much love and thanks!

FROM LESLIE STALL WIDENER

So much gratitude goes to my sister for the opportunity to tell this fascinating story in pictures. Celia, you inspire me every day. And to Terry and our children, a big thank you for your support during those late nights I spent at my drawing table.

TABLE OF CONTENTS

I

WHY WOULD ANYONE WEAR THAT?

"Clothes are never a frivolity; they are always an expression of the fundamental social and economic pressures of the time."
Laver (1968, p. 10)

What is a fashion? Many researchers study the term and offer definitions of varying lengths and scholarship. Simply put, a fashion is a style with group acceptance. Before a style can be transformed into a fashion, it requires a group of people to adopt it. An opinion leader may wear a certain style of clothing that appeals to the followers in his or her social circle, but the clothing may only be described as that individual's style until others choose to adopt the same look. Without imitation, there is no fashion.

Those who study fashion may define fashion as "change." When the newness of a fashion wears off; when its life cycle is complete, it is no longer considered a fashion. Fashion is the here and now; what is "in" today. The following centuries-old excerpt from an English play titled *Rhodon and Iris* (1631) describes the time-tested human preoccupation with desiring the most current and popular styles. The author refers to seemingly fickle changes in headwear fashions: From coronets to plumed hats to coiffed hair.

Dress of a lady of fashion in the seventeenth century:
Wear a flowing coronet to-day, the symbol of her beauty's sad decay;
To-morrow she a waving plume will try, the emblem of all female levity,
Now in her hat, now in her hair is drest;
Now, of all fashions, she thinks change the best.
(Reprinted in Chambers, 1832, p. 42)

Victim of fashion or fashionista? Fanciful or functional? What makes men and women adopt ridiculous styles in the name of fashion? Have people always been free to choose what they wear? Are the wearers themselves at fault for adopting these fashions? Do *victims of fashion* really exist?

We cannot ignore the social pressures that demand and dictate conformity in clothing, and we cannot simply blame followers of fashion for making foolish clothing choices. Fashion conformity is especially noticeable in secondary schools filled with teenage students. Adolescents shop at select stores and wear certain brands because these styles project a desired image. Dozens of students may own similar T-shirts or pairs of jeans because it reinforces their identity and reaffirms group acceptance. Teens may avoid looking different from their peer group, because it can be a fateful sentence of isolation.

Some people wear luxurious and expensive apparel and accessories so others might be impressed with their show of money. Conspicuous consumption is the social concept describing the deliberate, outward expression or display of one's wealth. The economist Thorstein Veblen coined the term "conspicuous consumption," in the early twentieth century, although the desire to flaunt one's wealth has always been a part of the fabric of civilization. The author Diana Crane explained the appeal of fashion as follows:

> The seductiveness of fashion, then as now, lay in the fact that it seemed
> to offer a person the possibility of becoming in some way different, more
> attractive, or more powerful.
> (2000, p. 67)

In some societies, the ultimate show of prosperity is for an affluent person to have so much money that he or she appears to be incapable of engaging in physical labor. By the nineteenth century, the appearance of aristocratic idleness or conspicuous leisure lacked practicality for the male head of the household, as the primary breadwinner, so the wife became the home's chief ornament. The unofficial ruler of English fashion, George Bryan "Beau" Brummel identified the trend toward male conservatism when he stated, "The less a gentleman is noticeable, the more he is elegant" (Miller, 1999, p. 28).

Although the popularity of men dressing like dandies waned during the nineteenth century, constrictive clothing for women continued to symbolize the leisure class. Wealthy families could pay for every imaginable service—a servant to choose clothes, a servant to button dresses and coif hair, and even a servant to aid her in walking.

Historically, extreme fashions may have been uncomfortable or difficult to wear, and in some instances, the fashions were forced on the wearer. Some of the following pages cite historical instances when parents subjected their children to deforming and painful styles in the name of fashion. Wealthy or elite citizens often advocated physical disfigurement in the name of beauty, fashion, or social status. By contrast, working class and poor people needed their children to work to help pay for basic necessities. These people required functional clothing for performing routine activities; cumbersome clothing was simply not practical.

Carefully crafted laws officially regulated the wearing of certain fashions, while simple economics often determined who wore other types of clothing. The time and money restrictions on the lower-class citizens prevented them from investing excessively in fashion frivolities. They needed comfortable and easy-to-wear clothing that allowed them the freedom of movement to earn a living. In spite of these limitations, people from lower socio-economic classes often imitated fashions or popular styles. As students of fashion read through the historic styles discussed in this book, they should bear in mind that only a limited number of men and women adopted the most extreme fashions—and usually, they were of the leisure class.

Clothing symbolizes power in most societies. The more extensive (larger, wider, taller, or longer) or expensive the fashion, the more status and power bestowed upon the wearer. Thus, extremely tall hats, wide skirts, costly and excessive fabrics, and precious jewelry create a feeling of power, but when the fashion becomes so cumbersome that it prevents freedom of movement, the wearer's physical or perceived power declines. Instead, the person becomes a victim of the very fashion he or she freely chose to wear.

In spite of all the theories and perspectives of fashion adoption, there is an important underlying reason why extreme fashions are worn—for adornment or to attract attention. People simply want to adorn themselves so they will be attractive to others.

This book explores historic fashion extremes across time and place, and literally from head to toe, by beginning with headwear fashions and concluding with footwear fashions. Students of fashion will find that while a few extreme fashions offered benefits to the wearer, many others ranged from uncomfortable to downright dangerous or deadly.

II
FASCINATING FASHIONS

HENNINS

Europeans living in the fourteenth and fifteenth centuries emphasized religion. The cathedrals dominated the towns and cities, and the church controlled much of society's wealth. Art, architecture, and even clothing emphasized heavenly aspirations. Church paintings depicted religious scenes and biblical stories. Elaborate cathedrals featured high pointed arches rising toward the heavens. Slender and vertical clothing fashions gave a similar illusion of piousness. Women of wealth in France donned a conical hat, called a hennin, which resembled a church steeple. To achieve a clean look, a woman might pull her hair up in a tight bun and pluck the hairs above the forehead, so none showed under her hat. As with many fashions, the hennin first appeared in moderate height, but with its growth in popularity came a growth in proportion and ornamentation, such as floor-length transparent scarves draped from the pinnacle. A woman's rank in society determined the height of her hennin. The more social power enjoyed by a woman's family, the higher her hennin—sometimes as high as four feet!

MAD AS A HATTER

Remember the Mad Hatter in Englishman, Lewis Carroll's *Alice's Adventures in Wonderland?* In the 1800s, some makers of felt hats indeed went mad as a result of mercury nitrate poisoning. Prolonged exposure and the inhalation of mercury fumes from the chemicals caused violent twitching and derangement—symptoms of a brain disorder. People often joked of a hatter's "drunkenness", which included a loss of hearing, slurred speech, trembling, stumbling, and memory loss. Mercuric poisoning was sometimes called the Mad Hatter's Syndrome, the Hatter's Shakes, or the Danbury Shakes, so named because Danbury, Connecticut, was a US hatmaking center.

FEATHERED HATS

The dawning of the twentieth century brought extravagance and controversy. By 1908, women's hat crown circumferences increased enormously to accommodate the large, upswept pompadour hairstyles. The hat surface left ample space for decorative masses of feathers and flowers. Milliners (mĭl-ĭn-ers) or hatmakers stuffed and mounted bird plumage and even whole bodies of small birds and creatures on spectacular fashion hats. This fashion trend resulted in the near extinction of several species of birds, including the snowy egret. Concerned US citizens organized chapters of the National Audubon Society, named after John Audubon, the famous ornithologist and illustrator of birds of North America. Members of the conservation groups protected endangered species of birds by insisting on legislation that outlawed usage, or at the very least, discouraging the wearing of plumage.

COWBOY HATS

Western cowboys were an entirely different group of hatwearing Americans, but were contemporaries of the fashionably hatted ladies. Cowboy attire served a functional purpose of protection from the elements. Western hats kept the sun and rain out of cowboys' eyes and off their necks; kept their heads warm or cool; and in a pinch, served as watering vessels for their horses. American cowboys adopted the hat style from their Mexican counterparts in the nineteenth century and the cowboy hat soon became a symbol of the Great American West.

A ten-gallon hat refers to a western hat with a large crown. Many believe the name represented the exaggerated crown size. However, some argue the Americans derived the term from *galón*, the Spanish word meaning gold braid (braid trim around the lower crown).

Occasionally, the western hat becomes a widespread fashion accessory. It embodies a sense of ruggedness and masculinity—unless, of course, it is colorful and embellished with rhinestones. In this case, it serves a nonfunctional purpose: Fashion adornment.

POWDERING

When artists portray the first president of the United States, George Washington, he is often featured wearing a powdered wig. Hair powdering was an acceptable fashion for both genders and a powerful symbol of an elite group. Women of leisure spent hours at the hairdresser, while artisans created incredible hair updos with false hair, Spanish moss, and flour paste (the consistency of a *papier maché* solution). Current events or the latest gossip inspired the bizarre creations for fashionable hair styles. Whether real or caricatures of the time, artwork from the century shows an upswept hairdo featuring a miniature sailing ship riding the crest of hair waves, and a hairdo that incorporates a miniature carriage and formal garden.

With so much time and expense invested in these *coiffures* (kwa-fures) or hairdos, it was desirable to maintain them for many days or even weeks. Some leisure-class citizens of the eighteenth century endorsed low hygiene standards and enterprising hairdressers devised long scratching sticks, so women could satisfy itches without mussing their hair.

The Scottish poet Robert Burns, sitting in the church pew behind a hatted woman with a coiffed hairdo, composed a poem titled *To a Louse* in 1786. Burns watched a louse scuttle on her head, disappearing in and out of her hairdo, while he wrote of his outrage at the audacity of the louse to crawl on such a well-dressed lady. An excerpt follows:

Ye ugly, creepin, blastit wonner,
Detested, shunned by saunt an' sinner,
How daur ye set your fit upon her,
Sae fine a lady!
Gae somewhere else and seek your dinner,
On some poor body.[1]

[1] *The poetical works of Robert Burns.* (1873). Boston: Lee and Shepard, pp. 120–121.

SCENTED CONES

If you lived in a very hot climate, would you be willing to shave your head? In ancient Egypt, many men and women sported smoothly shaved heads or very short hair to keep cool. Shaved heads also meant people prevented the common problem of head lice infestations.

In public, Egyptians often sported fancy wigs made of real hair, animal wool, or plant fibers. One of the most unusual wigs featured a headpiece to hold an orange-sized, scented beeswax cone. As the night progressed, the cone slowly melted, oozing fragrant rivulets of oil down the wearer's head and shoulders. Some ancient wall paintings show a golden yellow color on the shoulders of the Egyptians that may have represented melted cones.

Egyptians stored their moisturizing *unguents* (ointments) in tiny jars called *caskets,* and applied moisturizers regularly to prevent the hot and dry climate from parching their skin. This ancient culture viewed cosmetic application as a social activity for festive occasions. Similar to ancient civilizations, a group of modern-day teenage girls may still gather at one of their homes to fix their makeup and hair for a dance or the prom.

RUFFS

The ruff fashions originated from the modest neck ruffles on shirts for men and women in the latter half of the sixteenth century, about the same time starch was invented. Fashion historians may view numerous examples of ruffs on portraits of Spanish, Italian, French, and English men and women. Ruffs were commonly white or faintly tinted starched lengths of linen fabric shaped into stiff, deep ruffles. As the decades progressed, the ruffs increased in height and width, sometimes requiring decorative wire frames to support them. Beautiful embroidery or laces adorned the ruffs, which were artfully arranged in deep figure eight scallops. The cartwheel ruff fashion grew to extreme proportions before its fashion demise in the late 1620s. As is the case with all extreme fashions, the ruff became passé. Flattened wide linen or lace collars continued to be fashionable, standing high in the back and hanging down in the front. Eventually, the collar fashions evolved into a flat, draped capelet covering the expanse of shoulders. Traditional clergy in the Anglican Church may still be seen wearing a modest ruff.

THE HOPE DIAMOND

Driven by a compulsion to possess tiny bits of shiny stone that were
(at least until the advent of technology) utterly useless in themselves, men
have crossed oceans and deserts, scaled mountains and dived beneath the
surface of the sea; they have schemed and plotted, lied and stolen, fought wars
and suffered agonies of torture; they have killed and they have been killed.
(O'Neil, 1983, pp. 21–22)

Few gemstones boast a history as colorful and legendary as the Hope Diamond. Purported to be cursed for all who own it, the near flawless, steel blue Hope Diamond now resides peacefully in the Smithsonian Institute in Washington DC, encircled by 16 white diamonds. According to Hollywood legend, the 112-carat diamond's first home was the eye of a Hindu goddess. After it was stolen by a greedy priest, the angry goddess decreed that whoever wore her eye as jewelry would be cursed.

Beginning in the seventeenth century, a series of owners, legal and illegal, re-cut and named the large diamond the French Blue stone. Rumors indicated that multiple French kings died after wearing it. In 1830, the British Lord Henry Thomas Hope purchased the 44.5-carat stone. Although he died of natural causes, his unfaithful wife, a frequent wearer of the stone, was not so fortunate. The stone changed hands several more times and bad luck continued to plague subsequent owners. Finally, the New York jewelry magnate Harry Winston purchased the stone and donated it to the Smithsonian Institute, where it now rests peacefully for all to admire.

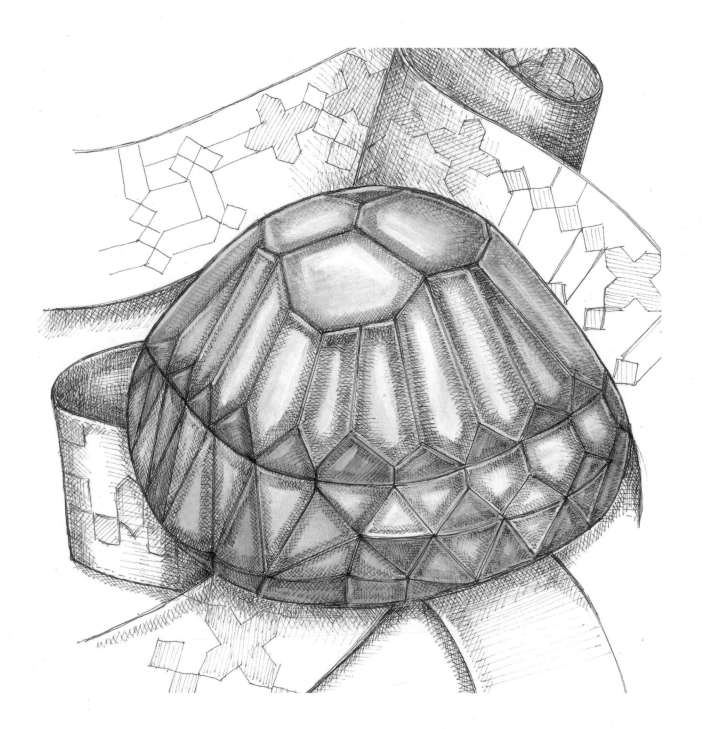

THE KOH-I-NOOR DIAMOND

An Afghan prince once owned another of the world's most famous and largest diamonds, the Koh-i-Noor Diamond. Amid controversy of ownership, it now resides in a platinum crown among the British crown jewels in London.

Like the Hope Diamond, the Koh-i-Noor Diamond possesses a tempestuous ancient history. Gemstone historians claimed the lackluster 105 carat diamond possibly influenced the fate of its owners. Some authorities believe the bloody history of this diamond can be traced back 5000 years. The legend tells of a greedy Persian invader, Nadir Shah, who plotted to steal the stone from an acquaintance, Muhammad Shah, who secretly kept the stone in his turban. Upon discovery of the hiding place, Nadir arranged a celebration banquet for Muhammad Shah. During the banquet, Nadir Shah proposed a gesture of benevolence and mutual respect that included trading turbans. Good breeding made a refusal by Muhammad Shah unthinkable. The men exchanged headwear and when Nadir Shah unwound Muhammad's turban, out tumbled the diamond. Nadir Shah exclaimed, "Koh-i-noor!" (*mountain of light*). To this day, Koh-i-Noor is the official name of the diamond.

GIRAFFE WOMEN

Were these Burmese women born with long necks? Cultural photographers have published many images of Burmese women wearing permanent stacks of brass or copper neck rings and armlets. To obtain a long-necked appearance, parents placed neck rings and arm and leg bands on their daughters' bodies (when they were around five years old) while the girls' bones were still being formed. Additional rings were added on a regular basis, the weight forcing their collarbones (clavicles) and ribs to grow at a downward angle and arm bones and muscles to develop around the bands. As the children matured, their arm muscles grew on either side of the armlets, causing tourniquet-like appearances on the upper arms.

Social historians ponder the origins of this type of body disfigurement. It may have once been a sign of wealth and leisure, although the rings are now typically brass or copper. The women who continue this practice believe they appear most beautiful when their necks are long. The pushed-up chin gives an elegant impression of a tiny head floating on a golden stem. While the practice has been criticized, it has also been called a sign of beauty, a commitment to the culture and tradition, and testament to personal choice. Examples of this practice still exist in Southeast Asia, between Burma (Myanmar) and Thailand.

MUSLIN FEVER

In the late 1700s, excavation took place on two ancient Greek cities buried by the eruption of the Mount Vesuvius volcano in 79 AD. France's Emperor Napoleon Bonaparte sent military campaigns to the bounteous ruins near Naples, Italy. Ancient marble vases and statues depicted women in white clothing (often the original color had completely worn off the artifacts). The profitable excavation of the thriving cities of Herculaneum and Pompeii set off a European fashion trend for the diaphanous (dī-ă-fa-nous) flowing and sheer look of a Greek goddess.

To achieve the Greek statue look, French women chose muslin or other filmy fabrics for dresses and wore pink tights underneath to give the illusion of bare skin. In extreme cases women chose to dampen the fabric to achieve the clinging look. Church officials criticized the lightweight fashions not just because of their revealing nature, but also because the wearers could easily succumb to influenza. The health epidemic of the times was referred to as muslin fever.

In addition to the sheer gauzy fabrics, important fashion trends included masses of curls, headbands, the color white, low necklines, and short puffed sleeves. Fashion historians refer to the raised waistline as the *Empire* (em-pīre or om-peer) waist because the style gained popularity during the Napoleonic Empire.

BURQAS

A burqa is not fashion; it represents an extreme style worn because of moral or religious principles. A burqa (burr-ka) is a cloak-like garment that completely envelops a woman's form, covering her from head to toe. A burqa includes a mesh facial screen that conceals a woman's eyes; she can see through the mesh screen, but outsiders cannot see her eyes. Islamic women may wear burqas in public places, although they are not required to do so in the privacy of their own homes.

The controversy usually surrounding the burqa involves the forced versus voluntary wearing of the garment. Proponents of the burqa say it represents religious piety and liberation. Opponents of the burqa insist it is a symbol of women's servitude and degradation. While considerable disagreement exists about the complex symbolism of burqas, there are several explicit reasons why women wear burquas. In some volatile regions of the world, such as the Middle East (Afghanistan, Iraq, Saudi Arabia), military governments have ordered women to wear burqas in public. Husbands may insist that their wives wear them, or women may willingly wear them for moral or religious reasons. Woman may feel modest and protected from sexual harassment when wearing the shroud-like garment because it conceals their bodies. Women may claim that a burqa demonstrates extreme piety or closeness to God. Still other women have stated that burqas liberate their minds because their earthly form cannot be judged by others. Critics of government-enforced burqa-wearing say the concealing garments symbolize subjugation or submission to men. Stronger critics liken the burqas to coffins, and condemn burqas because the garments deny the existence of the women and keep women in a state of isolation.

ZOOT SUITS AND TEDDY BOYS

Fads are short-lived fashions with a quick rise to popularity and an even quicker demise. Young, hip American men popularized the baggy zoot suit during the late 1930s and early 1940s. Zoot suits featured an oversized look: Exaggerated jacket length and wide, draped pants that tapered to tight ankle cuffs. African American jazz musicians wore the flowing zoot suits, which rippled with movement during jazz concerts. Soon, the Mexican American youth adopted the draped garment in defiance of the establishment and the government's wartime fabric rationing. Riots occurred in Los Angeles between the zoot suit wearers and military or police personnel. Newspapers reported on incidents of riots in which zoot suit pants were ripped off young men, and other acts of aggression that escalated during the "Zoot Suit Riots" of 1943.

By the 1950s, a British youth subculture called the Teddy Boys adopted styles similar to the draped zoot suit. Historians suggest that the clothes were loose interpretations of the Edwardian-era styles and the name "Teddy" is a variation of "Edward."

Photographs of Teddy Boys depict young men in thigh-length suit jackets, sometimes trimmed with velvet fabric on the collar, lapels, and pocket edges or flaps. If a Teddy Boy opted for a necktie, it would be narrow in order to complement the long, narrow shawl collar or lapel. The stovepipe (or drainpipe) pants legs created a slender silhouette, which was a change from the baggy-pants style of the zoot suits from the earlier decade. Efforts were taken to polish the bad-boy look by combing their hair forward and styling their heavy bangs.

LEISURE SUITS

While zoot suits and Teddy Boy outfits were fads among a limited group of young men, the early 1970s leisure suits gained widespread popularity among males of all ages. Leisure suits were casual, unstructured jackets with matching bell-bottom slacks. Manufacturers usually produced leisure suits in pastel colors and added contrasting and bold topstitching to ornament lapels, sleeve cuffs, and pocket flaps. A popular fabric for leisure suits was polyester double knit in peacock colors of yellow, blue, green, and lavender. Contrasting solid-color or decorative print shirts of polyester interlock knit complemented the ensembles.

The end of the 1960s ushered in the popularity of unisex clothing and colorful fashions for men, and helped blur gender distinctions. Suits continued to remain a staple of men's wardrobes, but the leisure suits took on effeminate proportions unseen in menswear for nearly two centuries. Fashion historians refer to this period as the "peacock revolution."

BREAST BINDING

The 1920s was a time of women's emancipation in the western world. Fashions included shortened skirts, bobbed (short) haircuts, flapper dresses, and a rise in the popularity of physical activity for women. After the previous decades of large bosoms, tiny waists, and curvaceous female forms, the fashion pendulum swung decidedly in the opposite direction. Women achieved the flat-chested, boyish or *garçon* (gair-sown) look by practicing breast binding. In addition, the dropped waistline fashion of the time created a tubular silhouette.

Historians credit the French couture designer Coco Chanel with popularizing all kinds of costume jewelry during the 1920s. Regardless of socio-economic class, women wanted the must-have fashion of knotted pearl ropes or multiple strands of pearls. Designers and fashion magazines encouraged frugal consumers to wear ropes and ropes of real, or *faux* (fō) or fake pearls. Breast-binding became a fad to ensure the pearl ropes swung freely across the torso.

FLEA FURS

The late fourteenth century brought the unimaginable horror of the Great Plague. Historians estimate the deadly bubonic plague wiped out one-third of the European population. Tiny fleas carried the disease that spread quickly across Europe as flea-carrying seaport rats moved from ship to ship and harbor to harbor. Wealthy Europeans fled to their country estates, away from the masses and the filth of the cities. Outbreaks of the bubonic plague continued for decades and into the subsequent century. One wonders if this terrible plague may have given rise to the flea fur fashion that occurred more than a century later.

During the mid-to-late sixteenth century, affluent women carried a fashion accessory known as a flea fur or zibellini, which was the entire pelt of a fur-bearing animal, such as a sable or mink. Many portraits of elegant ladies depict them holding a limp, furry creature. Fashion historians may speculate as to the precise purpose of these perplexing fashion accessories. Were flea furs intended to attract fleas and keep them off the elegant ladies? While an interesting idea, this would not have worked. Modern scientists know that fleas are only attracted to warm-blooded living animals, not dead ones. Were flea furs a form of a flexible fur muff to wrap around a woman's cold hands? Were they a symbol of the pecuniary (having to do with wealth) culture, since only the wealthy could afford furs?

History tends to repeat itself: Entire fur-bearing animals have been worn by fashionable ladies of the twentieth century, too. As recently as the 1950s, fox, sable, or mink skins, complete with ears and face, legs and feet, and long bushy tails could be seen draped around the shoulders of fashionable women. A spring clip secured beneath the animal's head clasped the head to the tail, so the fur pelt would remain secure around the woman's shoulders.

CORSETS

Although most people associate corsets with women's clothing, men have also adopted corsets to create an hourglass fashion look. Early in history, undergarments served to keep the wearer warm, to protect the skin from uncomfortable outerwear, and to protect the outerwear from body oils and perspiration. By the seventeenth century, an undergarment might also function to shape the body. Corsets created a tiny wasp waist, which has been a recurring fashion theme for over 3000 years. Although a narrow waist was the result of corseting, the focal point became the exaggerated appearances of the chest and hips above and below the contraption.

Unfortunately, tightly-laced corsets created medical problems for young women, whose parents corseted them before adolescence. Problems included fainting, shortness of breath, reproductive difficulties, malformed internal organs, constipation, indigestion, and headaches. A few extremists opted for surgically removing the lower ribs to create an even smaller waistline. A small waist symbolized the social elite, and men and women willingly endured these physical difficulties so that they could acquire the status associated with membership of the leisure class.

CAGED CRINOLINES

The Victorian era corresponded to the reign of England's Queen Victoria I during the latter half of the nineteenth century. The queen modeled the important social behaviors of the day, including morality and modesty. Women's skirts became increasingly cumbersome, with numerous layers of petticoats needed to achieve a full look. While the extreme width of the skirt fashion served as a physical barrier to keep men at a proper Victorian distance, some fashion historians say the restrictive fashion also resulted in a type of female bondage.

From a favorable perspective, the invention of the caged crinoline or hoop skirt eliminated the discomfort of layers of heavy petticoats. It allowed a woman's legs to be more mobile, although the hoop skirt circumference limited her ability to travel. It also acted as a power extender by allowing a generally powerless woman to increase her personal space.

The caged crinoline created a demand for even wider skirt fashions and a new set of problems accompanied the giant hoop skirts. How did a woman ride in a confined area, such as public transportation or a carriage? How could she get through doorways? How could she control the swing of her voluminous skirt? How could she keep from knocking things off tables as she passed? How could she relieve herself? Clever solutions included kneeling pads for short carriage rides; enlarging doorways; a ban on hoops at functions with open gas heating flames; decorative table railings; and bifurcated chemises (or undergarments) with an unsewn crotch seam.

The widespread popularity of the caged crinoline—across oceans and social classes—was achieved by mass production techniques. Clothing producers used the newly-invented sewing machine to aid in the mass production of the full skirts and steel factories supplied the steel needed to manufacture the hoops.

BUSTLES

In a costume history class, students usually learn that there are three major categories of skirt silhouettes: Tubular or straight; bell or bouffant; and back fullness. Throughout history, each silhouette has experienced periods of rising popularity, mass acceptance, and declining popularity. Such was the case in the nineteenth century when the bustle or back-fullness style almost exclusively dominated women's fashions. In the late 1860s, the bustle fashion began as upswept fabric that created an enlarged derriere with a moderate amount of back fullness.

Advertisements of 1869 referred to the item as a *dress improver*. The bustle may have been a fashion relief from the previously popular caged crinolines, but it was not so different when it was first introduced. The original dress improver's appearance can be described as half of a caged crinoline—the back half. This new style simplified manufacturing alterations and offered women a change, though it was not drastically different from the full caged crinoline. Over the years, the bustle moved precise locations; became more of a belted-on basket; and generally evolved to ensure continuous interest in the changing scenario of women's fashions. Subsequent years revealed a growing extension of the bustle and by the end of its fashion life cycle, the bustle reached exaggerated proportions, resembling a back shelf.

CHASTITY BELTS

The protective garment known as a chastity belt was never a "popular" item, therefore officially it cannot be deemed a fashion. The sixteenth-century chastity belts were padlocked metal contraptions of varying designs, attached, more or less permanently, around a woman's lower torso and genitals to prevent her from having sexual intercourse. It was intended to keep a young, unmarried woman a virgin until her wedding day or prevent a married woman from having sexual intercourse with anyone but her husband while he was away for an extended period of time. Given the wearer's discomfort and unsanitary nature of a chastity belt, it seems highly unlikely that a woman would willingly choose such a device.

Now, consider a contrasting scenario in which a woman might intentionally wear a chastity belt. During the eighteenth and nineteenth centuries, young women often found employment in factories where they might be subjected to sexual harassment by their male supervisors. Perhaps these women found it safer to don a locking chastity belt before work each day, than to experience rape by sexual predators.

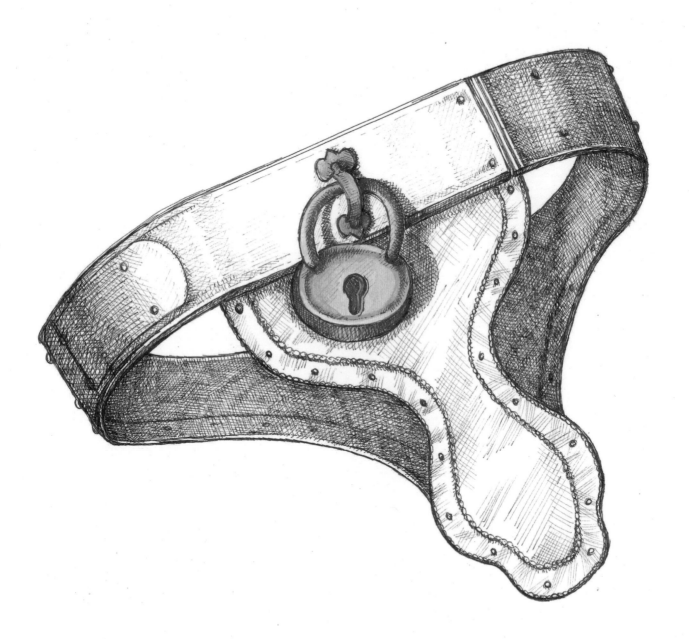

BLOOMERS

The Union Army commissioned Dr. Mary Edwards Walker as an assistant surgeon during the American Civil War. Dr. Walker lobbied for a woman's right to wear clothing of her choice. She originally chose to wear full Turkish trousers, gathered at the ankles, under long tunics. She advocated that choice of clothing influenced a woman's mental and physical health and that good health was hampered by the wearing of corsets. During Dr. Walker's lifelong crusade, law enforcement officials arrested her for impersonating a man, because some laws forbade women to claim social equality with men. As she grew older, her clothing became increasingly masculine and many of Mary Walker's contemporaries felt threatened by her strange ideas and behaviors.

In spite of the initial resistance to her revolutionary attire, fashionable women eventually adopted modified versions of her style. By the early twentieth century, active women adopted divided skirts or bifurcated (having two legs) apparel for day wear. A recognizable bifurcated item bears the name of the feminist who made the style famous—Amelia Bloomer. Although named for Amelia Bloomer, the real popularity of bloomers can be traced back to the invention of the bicycle. Bicycle riding in a long skirt was a dangerous occupation, so a bifurcated skirt with tighter legs became necessary. Bicycling made its appearance first as an upper-class leisure activity and later it trickled down to the masses.

PUMPKIN BREECHES

Men's trouser legs gradually widened, narrowed, and widened again over a 60-year time span, with the 1660s marking their bulkiest point. Pumpkin breeches and petticoat breeches emerged as two different, but similar fashions of the time and were mostly popular with younger men. As is often the case, older adults tended to dress in more conservative and less bulky styles, leaving the extreme fashions to the more youthful.

The legs of pumpkin breeches resembled the shape of pumpkins. They were voluminous pants with full, rounded legs created from multiple layers of interlinings. Petticoat breeches featured bunched or looped ribbon decorations around the lower edge that resembled the trim on women's undergarments. The underlining of the petticoat breeches hung below the hem edge of the fashion fabric. Before the fashion waned in popularity and a more conservative style emerged, dozens of yards of colored ribbons were looped and knotted on the legs of the breeches and on matching waistcoats.

HOBBLE SKIRTS

Critics say fashion can be counter-productive to social progress, because it encourages women to willingly choose clothing that restricts their physical movement. While women's rights activists, called suffragettes, marched and picketed to gain women's voting rights in the US, the hobble skirts of 1910 caused extreme mobility restrictions—pseudo bondage—for women. The hobble skirts became so tight around the ankles that women could do little more than hobble as they walked. Was the hobble skirt a final effort to physically restrain women lest they become psychologically emancipated or was it an extreme swing of the fashion pendulum? Either way, the fad was short-lived and US women earned the right to vote in 1920.

POISON RINGS

Jewelry may signify various meanings that include adornment, symbolism, association, unity, and membership, but what about suicide or murder? While poison (or pillbox) rings might appear to be another case of adornment, their purposes were actually very deadly. The setting of the ring opened to expose a small space, which might contain cyanide or some other deadly poison. Persons caught spying might quickly consume the contents and die immediately, lest they be tortured. Assassins might secretly slip the poison into the drink of the intended victim without detection.

CODPIECE

The purpose of fashion may be to accentuate an erogenous zone or area of the body that represents sexuality. Students of fashion learn that a fashion commonly begins in small proportions, but by the end of the fashion life cycle, it reaches extreme proportions. Unquestionably, the sixteenth-century European codpiece, an ornamental cover for a man's genitals, represented an exaggerated fashion. Made of precious metals and encrusted with jewels, men who wore the codpiece attracted stares and attention towards their sex organs. The codpiece began as a functional pouch with a lacing closure between the legs of men's hosiery. By the conclusion of its life cycle, the codpiece had become a bulbous, ornamented, or padded focal point.

While genitals have been a fashion focal point on numerous occasions in world history, the codpiece represents an extreme fashion that was impossible not to notice!

PARTI-COLORED HOSIERY

Generally, fashion designers choose a dominant color scheme for clothing designs and then use accent colors to add visual interest. In the fourteenth century, a fashion trend emerged in which clothing was parti-colored or equal parts of two colors. Each noble family had its colors and heraldic motifs, such as a bird or *fleur de lis*. A marriage alliance brought together colors and icons from the bride's and groom's families into a single household. Both the nobility and the servants dressed in the dual motifs and bi-colored clothing to show their loyalty to the families of the husband and wife. Garments might be equally divided into halves or quarters, each one bearing a family motif or color. Artists of the time commonly painted bi-colored hosiery on men. Historic paintings show men's hosiery with one leg in one color and the other leg in a different color, or each leg divided between two colors. As an example, think of the joker from a deck of playing cards. The joker's clothing and hosiery are parti-colored, that is, half one color and half another.

CHINESE LILY FEET

An old custom of some Chinese families involved the extremely painful activity of binding the feet of their young daughters. The lily foot shoes were tiny, highly arched footwear, three to four inches in length, with virtually no space for toes. From infancy, parents folded a daughter's toes under her feet and bound them tightly to the heels, making the girl's feet highly arched and approximately half their normal size. This caused great pain and made unassisted walking difficult. Sometimes, it resulted in the loss of toes and the onset of infection. A three-inch "golden lotus" foot was the ideal, while a four-inch "silver lotus" ranked slightly less desirable. Proponents of the lily foot fashion viewed it as a sign of wealth and beauty: a way to secure a suitable marriage; a practiced custom; and a commitment to the ancient culture. Social historians suggest that the Chinese lily foot also restricted the mobility of Chinese women, prevented them from engaging in physical labor, promoted the notion of the husband's wealth and the wife's economic uselessness, and provided an additional female erogenous zone for their husbands.

POULAINES OR CRACOWS

People have long believed that a person's shoes serve as a social indicator. Today, there are no laws governing the type of shoes worn in a certain social class, but in the late fourteenth and early fifteenth centuries in Europe, the length of shoes indicated a person's social and political rank.

The fifteenth-century poulaine or cracow was a flat, slipper-like shoe with an exaggerated length extending many inches beyond the natural toe. Shoe manufacturers filled the long toe with moss or dried grass to keep it rigid. Excessive lengths required the wearer to walk with a slight kicking motion, to avoid bending and stepping on the toes. Today, people might have similar experiences wearing swim fins while walking on dry land.

The more practical noblemen attached the flapping toes to gold or silver chains that were gartered around the knees. In a few instances, tiny silver bells, called "folly bells," adorned the tips. The following Mother Goose nursery rhyme describes the sound of these musical shoes: "Ride a cockhorse to Banbury Cross to see a fine lady upon a white horse, rings on her fingers and bells on her toes, she shall have music wherever she goes."

During this time, the social classes engaged in a "fashion competition" in which people tried to emulate the social classes above them. To inhibit competition, the nobles enacted mostly ineffective laws to prevent rich lower-class citizens from wearing certain styles reserved only for the ruling class. Sumptuary laws restricted clothing based on moral or religious grounds, but they also deliberately barred the newly rich merchant class from out-dressing the cash-strapped nobility. Sumptuary laws specified which furs, fabrics, trims, and colors could be worn and by whom. In the case of the poulaine, sumptuary laws governed maximum toe lengths for each level of society. For example, a French law decreed that commoners' shoe points could not exceed six inches in length; wealthy merchants, 12 inches; and noblemen, 24 inches. English law allowed the prince to wear shoe points as long as he liked. Thus, poulaines or cracows became a badge of rank. As with many extreme fashions, these hard-to-manage shoes symbolized aristocratic idleness and the leisure class. Most citizens could not afford to wear the impractical fashions and needed functional clothing that allowed them to work and be productive.

By the early sixteenth century, the fashion pendulum swung to the opposite side and splayed toe shoes replaced the long, slender poulaines. Historians refer to the excessively wide shoes as bearpaw, hornbill, or cowmouth shoes. As time progressed, the decoration increased to include cutting and slashing off the tops of the shoes until the fashion declined and the fashion focal point moved to another area of the body.

CHOPINES AND PATTENS

It is often said that necessity is the mother of invention. Imagine crossing muddy, filthy streets, regularly traversed by horses and cattle. People of both genders adopted practical overshoes called French pattens, which elevated the feet a few inches out of the muck and mire. As time progressed, a modified solution for maintaining pristine slippers emerged in the form of iron ring platforms attached to wooden soled shoes. Italian chopines or platforms were popular in cities like Venice and gradually took on a decorative and monstrous form. Heights of a few inches grew to several inches and became solid wood or cork covered with fine leather, velvet, trim, and braid. A wealthy lady required servants to assist her with walking and prevent her from toppling. Shoes that were once designed to create mobility in difficult conditions gave way to shoes that required constant assistance and prevented women from straying too far from home.

Platform chopines, from 8 to 18 inches high, were a visual testimony to the confines society put on the "fragile and dependent" gender. Just like the Chinese lily foot and the hobble skirt, chopines effectively limited mobility. Only the very wealthy could afford to be incapacitated, so the higher the heel, the higher the status. Not surprising, women fortunate enough to be able to move freely were considered to be of a lower status.

RUNNING SHOES

Consider the diverse designs in running shoes during the recent decades, ranging from ultra-thick, cushioned and padded soles to wafer-thin soled shoes. Creative shoe manufacturers offer a mix of fashion, technology and clever marketing to appeal to extreme and casual athletes. Notable shoe designs have included air pumps, to regulate the space in shoe soles and lessen the impact of jarring; gel pads and springs to absorb the shock from impact; and separate compartments for each toe and minimal cushioning between the foot and the tarmac. These shoes resemble a glove for the foot with only a thin layer of plastic for the soles. Given the diverse gamut of running shoes, athletes may wonder whether running shoe designs are more a product of marketing research and consumers' desire for change, than anatomical research.

DISPOSABLE FASHIONS

"Disposable fashions"—the term is new, but the idea can be traced back to a forward-thinking, nineteenth-century newspaper editor. "People will have more work done, will dress better, change oftener … The more work can be done … by means of machinery, the greater will be the demand. Men and women will disdain … a nice worn garment, and gradually we shall become a nation without spot or blemish" (Horace Greeley quoted in Japp, 1880, *Industrial Curiosities*, 142).

"Disposable fashions are usually trendy, inexpensive items that are meant to be worn for a single season and then discarded" (Stall-Meadows, 2011, p. 346). This term is often interchanged with the terms "fast fashions" or "high street fashions," which refer to inexpensive mass-market interpretations of designer styles. People who study fashion may perceive a slight difference in meaning between the terms "disposable fashion" and "fast/high street fashion." Disposable refers to the longevity of the fashion in the buyer's wardrobe, rather than the styling of the garment. Fast fashion or high-street fashion usually refers to the inexpensive knock-offs of designer originals. It would be possible for a fast fashion garment to be a classic style, rather than a short-lived fad, as long as it is an adaptation of a designer's original. In spite of these minor differences, one might argue that the more fashion-forward a disposable garment is, the sooner it will be discarded because it will be out-of-fashion.

III

INTERPRETING AND PREDICTING FASHION

Some fashion historians say the only really *new* thing in fashion is the people that wear it. But, will people ever wear these extreme fashions again? Perhaps they will in some modified way, but the exact movement of fashion is difficult to predict. We can say, with some certainty, that most fashions will not recur in exactly the same way as they once did. The differing environmental factors—political, social, cultural, and economic—shape the fashions to accurately reflect what is happening in all these areas. These influencing factors are the Zeitgeist or the spirit of the times. Fashion is a reflection of the way of life at a given time, but it is not easy to discern its meaning. In fact, identifying the meaning of fashion may be likened to an attempt to describe the air that we breathe. Yet, when students of fashion learn how to "read" the environment, they can also make educated guesses about the direction of fashion trends.

In what ways can students of fashion make educated guesses about future fashions? The answer is probably good news for most young people. Watch television and movies, go shopping, listen to music, and study print and electronic media. Analyze the individual components of fashion—color, silhouette, details, fabrics, and trims. It is easier to predict the parts of fashion rather than the whole. Look to the past for ideas, but do not try to copy it exactly. Fashions must be relevant to today's society.

BIBLIOGRAPHY

No author. (2012). *The invention of blue jeans by Levi Strauss & Co. in 1873*. Levi Strauss and Co. Retrieved from http://www.levistrauss.com/about/heritage/resources/students-teachers.

Blumer, H. (1969). Fashion: From class differentiation to collective selection. *The Sociological Quarterly, 10*(3), 275–291.

Brannon, E. (2010). *Fashion forecasting*. NY: Fairchild.

Burns, R. (1786). *To a louse*. Retrieved March 3, 2003, from http://www.netpoets.com.

Chambers, R. (ed.). (1832). *The book of days: A miscellany of popular antiquities*. London & Edinburgh: W & R Chambers.

Crane, D. (2000). *Fashion and its social agendas*. Chicago: University of Chicago Press.

Field, G. A. (1970 August). The status-float phenomenon—The upward diffusion of innovation. School of Business at Indiana University. *Business Horizons, 8*, 45–52.

Flugel, J. C. (1930). *The psychology of clothes*. London: Hogarth Press.

Frings, G. (1999). *Fashion from concept to consumer*. Upper Saddle River, NJ: Prentice Hall.

Haffner, C. & Lusitana, D. (1998). *Treasure! Secrets of the Hope Diamond* [videorecording]. NY: A & E Home Video.

Japp, A. H. (1880). *Industrial Curiosities: Glances here and there in the world of labour*. London: Marshall Japp & Company.

Knight, C. (1845). *Old England: A pictorial museum*. London: Charles Knight and Company.

Lasky, K. (1997). *She's wearing a dead bird on her head!* NY: Hyperion Books.

Laver, J. (1968). *Dandies*. London: Weidenfeld and Nicolson.

Miller, B. M. (1999). *Dressed for the occasion: What Americans wore, 1620–1970*. Minneapolis, MN: Lerner Publications Co.

Nystron, P. (1928). *Economics of fashion*. NY: Ronald Press Co.

O'Neil, P. (1983). *Planet Earth: Gemstones*. Chicago: Time Life Books.

Payne, B., Winakor, G., & Farrell-Beck, J. (1992). *The history of costume: From the ancient Mesopotamians through the twentieth century*. NY: Harper Collins.

Roach-Higgins, M., & Eicher, J. (1992). *Dress and identity. Clothing and Textiles Research Journal, 10*(4), 1–8.

Sapir, E. (1931, 1959). Fashion. In R. Seligman (ed.), *Encyclopedia of the Social Sciences, 6,* 139–144.

Simmel, G. (1904). Fashion. *International Quarterly, 10,* 130–155.

Sproles, G. B. (1982). *Perspectives of fashion*. Minneapolis, MN: Burgess Publishing.

Stall-Meadows, C. (2004). *Know your fashion accessories*. NY: Fairchild.

Stall-Meadows, C. (2011). *Fashion now: A global perspective*. Upper Saddle River, NJ: Pearson/Prentice-Hall.

Storm, P. (1987). *Functions of dress: Tool of culture and the individual*. Upper Saddle River, NJ: Prentice-Hall.

Tortora, P., & Eubank, K. (1989). *A survey of historic costume*. NY: Fairchild.

Veblen, T. (1912). *Theory of the leisure class*. NY: Macmillan.